CONTENTS

9016055754

I WANT TO KNOW...

What was it like before the telephone?

Paul Humphrey

Illustrated by Lynda Stevens

Evans

First published in this edition in 2011 by
Evans Publishing Group
2A Portman Mansions
Chiltern Street
London WIU 6NR

© Evans Brothers Limited 2011

www.evansbooks.co.uk

British Library Cataloguing in Publication Data:
A CIP catalogue record for this book is available from the British Library

ISBN: 9780237544911

Planned and produced by Discovery Books
Cover designed by Rebecca Fox

For permission to reproduce copyright material the author and publishers gratefully acknowledge the following: Ancient Art and Architecture Collection: page 10; Mary Evans Photo Library: pages 12, 18-19, 21; Robert Harding: page 27; istock: cover, page 29; Peter Newark's Western Americana: page 10; Alex Ramsay: page 17; Ann Ronan Picture Library: pages 8, 15, 25; Science Museum: page 22

Printed by Great Wall Printing Company in Chai Wan, Hong Kong, August 2011, Job Number 1672.

5

This is the communications room. The displays tell us how people sent messages before the telephone was invented.

Come with me and you'll find out...

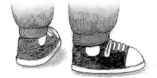

How do you think people sent messages to each other before telephones?

That's right. This picture shows a mail carrier. Hundreds of years ago, they delivered letters and parcels to people across Britain and Europe.

I bet it took them ages to deliver each letter.

But people sent messages even before that. They used drums to beat out the message.

Some of the Indian tribes
of North America used fire
to communicate. They sent
smoke signals.

Those are semaphore towers.
People could send messages from
one hilltop to another by raising
or lowering the arms.

Other people sent semaphore messages using flags.

But what happened if it was foggy?

No one could see the message.

14

That is a carrier pigeon. People would put messages into that little container on its leg. Then they would send it flying to the person receiving the message.

People wanted to send more complicated messages, so they made pens out of feathers. They sharpened the end and dipped it in ink and wrote their message.

17

A postal system was set up and letters and parcels were carried by stagecoach from one person to another.

In America, Pony Express riders galloped thousands of kilometres from one side of the country to the other.

I would like to have been a Pony Express rider!

It's a lantern for flashing out a message in code. It is called Morse Code.

A long flash is called a dash and a short flash is called a dot. Does anyone know any Morse Code?

Of course, you had to be able
to see the flashes of light
to get the message. The next
invention used electricity to
send the Morse Code message
along wires.

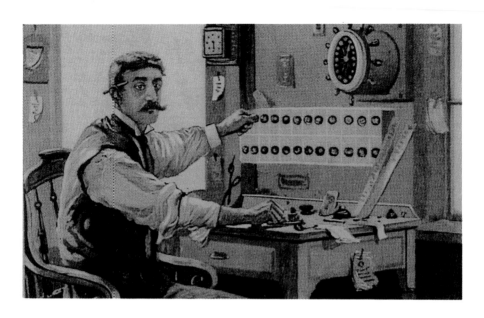

The telegraph operator would tap out a message on a transmitter like this one. But you still had to be able to read the code.

The next invention was a big step forward. It meant that messages could be sent over long distances and that people could just talk normally.
What was it?

That is what a very early
telephone looked like.

Today we can use the telephone to talk to people all over the world. With the internet we can also send written messages instantly using emails.

29

Fun activities

Can you remember how each of the things on this page were used to send messages? You will find the answers at the bottom on the page.

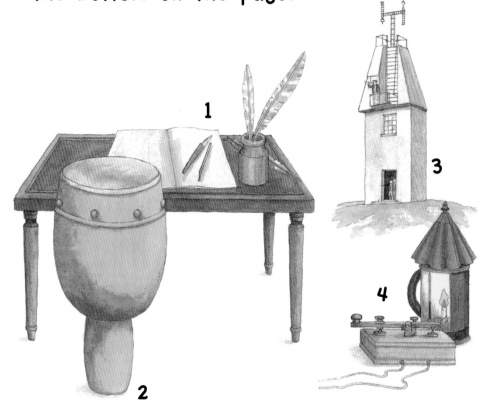

1 People made pens out of the feathers and dipped them in ink before writing their message.

2 Before letters people used drums to beat out messages.

3 Semaphore towers were used to send messages from one hilltop to another by raising or lowering the arms. Other people sent semaphore messages using flags.

4 Lanterns were used for flashing out messages in a code known as Morse Code. Transmitters were later used to send the Morse Code messages along wires.

Make your very own telephone!

YOU WILL NEED:

Two plastic cups

Long piece of string

A partner to help you

1. Ask an adult to make a hole in the bottom of each cup. Thread the end of the string through one of the holes. Tie a large knot in the end so that it doesn't fall back through. Repeat with the other cup, using the other end of the string.

2. Your telephone is now ready. Ask your partner to hold one of the cups to their ear. Standing as far apart as possible, speak into the other cup. Can they hear you? Take it in turns to speak and listen.

Imagine you are a carrier pigeon on a mission to deliver a very important and urgent message to someone. Write a passage describing your journey. What you see along the way? Do you encounter any difficulties? Do you manage to deliver the message safely and in time?

Interesting websites:

Have fun communicating through Morse Code. This website shows you the codes for each letter of the alphabet and numbers:
http://news.bbc.co.uk/cbbcnews/hi/newsid_4390000/newsid_4393400/4393451.stm

Learn more about messages through the ages:
http://www.birminghamstories.co.uk/story_page.php?id=7&type=fo&page=1&now=0

Explore the history of the Pony Express:
http://www.ponyexpress.org/history

Index